Navigating the Path to Industry:

A Hiring Manager's Advice for Academics Looking for a Job in Industry

D1056938

M. R. Nelson

AnnorlundaBooks

Published in the United States by Annorlunda Books. Queries:
info@annorlundaenterprises.com

First Edition

ISBN: 0990744523
ISBN-13: 978-0990744528

CONTENTS

INTRODUCTION

If you're reading this book, you are probably at least contemplating looking for a job outside academia. If you are like most people in academia, you are not sure how to conduct such a search. That is not your fault. Academia, at all levels, does not talk much about how to leave it.

That's where this book comes in. It is a collection of job searching advice distilled from more than ten years as a hiring manager, my own multiple job searches, and the advice I've been given over the years from friends, colleagues, and professional outplacement services.

My background is in the biomedical sciences and information technology. I have spent my career in the United States, primarily in the biotechnology and pharmaceutical industries. My advice is skewed towards my background, but it is tempered by information from friends in other fields and what I learned in general outplacement courses I have taken over the years. In general, the earlier portion of my advice is likely to be relevant to most industries, while the specific advice about resumes, cover letters and interviewing should be confirmed with someone in the industry that you are targeting. Don't worry, in the first part of this book, I'll talk about how to meet someone who can provide that confirmation.

In short, think of this book as providing a framework for your job search. It cannot guarantee you a job — unfortunately, nothing can do that. It also cannot provide a specific roadmap for your job search. You will need to fill in the details for yourself, based on your own particular skills and goals. It will, however, help you get started and give you a general idea of the steps you need to take and some common pitfalls to avoid.

The very first pitfall to avoid is waiting until you need a job to start the process of looking for one. A great deal of the work that goes into finding a job can be done well before you need one, and in fact, much of it is best done before you are ready to move on from your current situation. You can and should start some of the tasks described in this book even before you know what, exactly, you want to do next. This is because the most successful approach to finding a job is via an actual connection with a hiring manager. Building a network that will lead to that connection and developing the skills with which to follow up on that connection both take time. Do not despair if you are in the midst of an active job search and have not done the preparatory work I recommend in the first part of this book. You can jumpstart this work by focusing more time and effort on it now. However, if you are a year or more from the end of your academic position and think you have plenty of time before you need to worry about these things, I urge you to reconsider. Your eventual job search will be much easier if you start building a foundation for it now.

This book is divided into four parts. The first covers the preparatory work that you should do before you start to apply for jobs. Part two discusses the mechanics of applying for jobs. Part three offers some final thoughts on the job search process, and part four provides notes and links to additional resources.

PART I: PREPARE YOURSELF TO APPLY FOR JOBS

You may think that the most important thing to do in a non-academic job search is to find job postings and reply to them. This is not true. Your search is likely to be successful in less time if you do some preparatory work before you start. This section describes that work.

1. Lay the foundation

Set up your software and systems

The first thing to do is to make sure you have a neutral email address. It should not be tied to your university, because the hardest work in a job search is making new contacts, and you want those contacts to persist after you get your first job. If you are searching for a job in the United States, it should have a US domain name (e.g., ".com" and not ".co.uk"). Even if you have permanent residency, a non-US domain name may make potential employers and other contacts think you will require sponsorship. If you do need sponsorship, it is better to postpone that discussion until the other person has met you and formed some idea of how valuable your skills would be to his or her company.

The email address you use for your job search should be completely professional. Avoid using jokes or informal nicknames in the address. In general, it is best to try to get some version of your full name or first initial and last name. You do not need to move all of your correspondence to this email address; you can just forward the address to your main one, and log into your account only when you have emails to send.

The next thing to do is to decide what software you'll use to produce your key documents, such as your resumes and cover letters. If you are aiming at a field that requires giving a seminar or other presentation as part of the interview, you also need to consider how you will create your presentation materials (i.e., your slides). You should always send your resume to people as a PDF file, so that the formatting will be preserved and you can be certain they will be able to open it with software they already have. It does not matter what software you use to produce your resume, as long as that software is capable of doing basic formatting and can export the document as a PDF file. If you need to create presentation slides and are going to use anything other than the presentation software standard in your field (in most cases, Microsoft PowerPoint), then be sure that you can export to a PDF file and that you are comfortable running your presentation from a PDF file. In many cases, you can bring your own laptop and run your presentation from it, but sometimes you will be required to use the company's computer.

Next, you need to decide how you want to organize your job search information. You will make many new contacts, so decide upfront where you will store information about them. You certainly need to store contact information and a job title for each person you talk to about your career. You may also want to store a few notes about them so that you do not need to ask the same questions again when you reconnect with them in the future.

As you will see later, you will also generate a lot of resumes and cover letters — one for each job for which you apply. You absolutely must keep these organized, because accidentally sending the wrong cover letter to a company will almost certainly end your chances for that job. I personally have a set of folders on my computer for my cover letters and resumes, with one folder for each job for which I apply. I also have a notebook in which I keep a list of people I need to contact and other specific tasks for my job search. I use LinkedIn to maintain my list of contacts. I will discuss LinkedIn in more detail later in this book.

Prepare yourself mentally

The final piece of preparation is to make sure you are approaching the search with a strong and resilient mindset. This is the easiest preparation step to skip, but in many ways the most important to complete. Searching for a job is difficult even in the best of economic times, and these are not the best of economic times. There is no set script I can give you to prepare your mindset, but the following points might be helpful.

First, remember that you are only trying to find your first job. Your first job is not your forever job. It does not have to be the perfect manifestation of all your hopes and dreams. It just has to be interesting and rewarding enough for you to feel confident you'll stay at least a couple of years, and it should provide you with skills and experiences upon which you can continue to build. As unfair as it seems from your current position in academia, industry experience really does matter. Even if it doesn't matter from an "able to perform the job functions" point of view, it almost certainly matters from a "someone will decide to hire you" point of view. You will find it easier to get future jobs once you have industry experience, just because you have that experience. You will also have a wider network and a broader view of the various types of jobs available. So don't get hung up looking for the perfect job now. Look for a good job.

Even if you aren't aiming for the perfect job, a job search is a hard, ill-defined process that is almost guaranteed to humble you from time to time. Remember, it is hard for everyone. Don't lose faith in yourself. I have conducted several successful job searches over the course of my career, but I have never conducted one that did not involve rejection. You need to develop methods for maintaining your self-confidence and positive attitude in the face of the inevitable rejection. Potential techniques for this include: keeping a folder of positive feedback and evidence of your past successes to review when you are struggling, developing a closure routine to "say good-bye" to jobs you wanted but did not get, and practicing the "fake it until you make it" method of pretending to be more confident than you feel.

If a non-academic job search was not your first career choice, make sure that you can discuss the reasons you are looking for a job outside academia without bitterness before you start your search or start networking in support of your search. You may have every right to be extremely bitter about your time in academia and your reasons for leaving it. Hash that out with a counselor or your friends before you start your search. Networking contacts are not agony aunts. You will do your job search great harm if you unleash a rant about your past experiences on them. In fact, you will likely harm your job search if your description of what you've done and what you want to do contains even a hint of bitterness. This may not be fair, but it is true. Remember, you are trying to find a group of people who want to spend roughly 40 hours per week with you. Would you want to spend that much time with someone who spews venom about the past? Would you trust such a person not to spew venom about you in the future? Probably not. Do whatever it takes to purge any anger and bitterness from your discussions of your career plans.

If you are having trouble discussing your future plans without bitterness, it might help to focus on the benefits of working in industry. Salaries are usually higher, and there are often more safeguards in place to make sure that your work does not consume your life and that your supervisor and colleagues treat you fairly and professionally. It is usually easier to move between positions, making the option of leaving a toxic culture or disrespectful environment much less painful. And the work can be very rewarding. True, you are less likely to be pushing the frontiers of human knowledge forward (although some people working in industry do indeed do that), but you are more likely to see a direct, practical application of your work.

Conversely, if the reason that you are bitter is that you hated your time in academia, try instead to focus on the aspect of it that you most enjoyed, and, if at all possible, spend more time on that aspect than on others during the remainder of your time there.

Brush up on etiquette

Your job search will require many social interactions, both in person and online. If you have any doubts about proper etiquette in these interactions, address them before you start your search. Although you can almost always recover from an unintentional faux pas by giving a sincere and full apology, it is better to avoid mistakes if you can.

A full discussion of etiquette is beyond the scope of this short book. There are already many books on etiquette, but some key points are worth highlighting:

- Many established professionals make a practice of paying for the meal when they meet someone for a networking coffee or lunch. However, you should never expect this. Always expect to pay for your own food. If you can afford it, it is polite to offer to cover your networking contact's check as well. If you cannot afford it, simply do not mention money until the check arrives, and produce the money to pay for your meal.

- Always follow up after any networking meeting with a thank you email. Also send a thank you email if someone otherwise assists you in your search, for instance by introducing you to someone else who might be able to help you.

- Never relay someone's contact information to someone else without asking permission first. Simply send the first person an email asking for permission, and wait for a response before proceeding.

- If someone provides assistance with an active job search, it is nice to let that person know when you accept a job, and thank them again for their help in your search.

- Never say something about someone that you would not say directly to that person. This is doubly true on social media, where posts can spread far beyond their intended audience. Assume that anything you say about someone will eventually reach them, and be sure that you are happy to accept the consequences of that before you speak.

- If you decided to join new social media networks as part of your job search, take the time to watch the conversation for a while before engaging fully. This will help you learn what the expected standards and norms are in that network. You can also often find good online guides for "newbies" to various networks. Social media is not a consequence-free zone. Be sure that your behavior online reflects the standard by which you wish to be judged.

2. Figure out what to do

Before you can run a job search, you need an idea of what sort of jobs you want to find. Even if you think you already know what you want to do next, it is worth taking a little bit of time to explore other options. There are likely to be interesting and rewarding jobs that you have never even considered. Chances are, you've only heard about the jobs closest to your academic field. The problem is those are the same "alternative" careers that everyone in your field considers. It may prove easier to get hired in a job a little further from your academic field.

There are two approaches to identifying potential jobs: you can catalog your skills and look for jobs that match the skills you have, or you can identify interesting jobs and look at how your background might be relevant. I think the latter is likely to be more successful, but it might be easier to start with the former. However, you are likely to need to iterate through both approaches, so start wherever is most comfortable.

Identify your skills

Identify your skills using whatever brainstorming method works best for you. Write down all the skills you identify, even if they seem minor. You can winnow the list later. Consider all of your potentially relevant experiences, not just experiences for which you earned money or a grade. Have you organized projects? Led a team? Collaborated on a project? Include analytical skills you've picked up in your studies, and don't overlook the fact that you have probably developed the ability to write clear arguments and to structure and give presentations. If you have been involved in the administration of computers or other shared resources in your research group, be sure to include the skills developed as part of that work as well.

If your job search is still a year or two away, consider looking for volunteer or service opportunities that would give you some skills you haven't picked up in your studies. If you can find appropriate volunteer or service opportunities relevant to your target industry, these experiences might also allow you to meet people working in that industry. These people may turn out to be some of the most helpful members of your network, not just because they are in your target industry, but because they will know how well you work on a team, which is an important job skill.

Some volunteer opportunities are time limited, such as working on or organizing a conference, and some require only a few hours a week. Even so, not everyone can make time for unpaid volunteer work in their schedule. If you cannot, do not despair. You have accumulated many useful skills in your academic experience, you just need to shift your perspective and see them. Here is a list of skills you might have developed in your academic work:

- Analyzing a problem and independently developing ideas for possible solutions
- Teaching yourself about a new topic
- Teaching others about a topic
- Breaking the work in a large project into discrete tasks, and managing your time to ensure completion of the project (these are key project management skills)
- Collaborating productively with someone else, even without any formal authority to demand work from that collaborator (often called "consensus-building" in corporate-speak)
- Working productively with remote collaborators

- Writing clearly
- Clearly articulating a point of view about an issue.

This is not an exhaustive list. There are sure to be other general skills you can identify, as well as technical skills specific to your field of study.

Identify possible jobs

In order to match your skills to potential jobs, you need to have an idea of the sorts of jobs that are available. This is a chance to use the research skills you have developed in academia — you need to research the job market.

Start by reading job descriptions. Go to the websites of companies and other potential employers that interest you, click on the careers section and read the job descriptions. If there are a lot of jobs listed, you can use the search function to narrow the list, but it is better to read them all, particularly in the early stages of your research process. Your view of what jobs are available and worth considering has been limited by the filter of academia. You want to take off that filter and really consider all of the options.

If you don't know what specific websites to visit, you can start by running very general searches on job aggregator sites such as Monster.com. Those sites charge employers to run their postings, though, so some smaller employers might not list their jobs. Since you don't want to limit your research at this point, be sure to expand your search to include other sources, too. One way to identify potential employers is to think of a company whose products or services you like, and then go search their website.

Remember, you are not looking for jobs for which to apply at this point. You are looking for ideas about possible career paths, and entry-level jobs for which you have the necessary skills.

Also try to find professional societies that include people with your background and read their websites. Go to LinkedIn.com, search using keywords that describe your skills and experience, and read the job descriptions this finds. If you don't like the jobs your searches find, try describing your skills in a different way, and see if you find different jobs. This is also an easy way to gauge how your description of your skills will be perceived by people in your target industry, and gives you a chance to refine your message before you talk to anyone.

You can also search the web and see if you find any relevant blogs. You'll probably notice that there are far more academic bloggers than industry bloggers, but there may be some industry bloggers in your field, and the academic bloggers might occasionally write about how their work gets applied in industry.

Online research is a great tool, but you should also try to find some actual people to talk to about your career interests. If there are any industry networking events in your local area, go to them. If an interactive networking event seems too overwhelming at first, start with the events that are built around a lecture or panel discussion. These events often include a networking or social component before or after the main lecture or discussion. You can use the topic of the lecture to start a conversation with other attendees, or you can simply ask "what brings you here?" The line to get food or drinks is an excellent place to try to strike up conversations, since standing in line gives you an excuse to stand next to someone and start talking. Regardless of how you start the conversation, talk to people and see what they do.

Once you have identified some potential fields, you need to do more research to determine which ones you should really pursue. The best way to do this is via informational interviews, which are an aspect of networking. Networking is so important that it has its own section a little later in the book.

Learn the professional version of your field

Even if the field that you are targeting is a direct industrial equivalent of your academic field, you need to do some research. There are often differences in how that field is practiced in industry. It is common for the industrial version to focus more on reliability and less on bleeding edge innovation. People working in industry don't generally expect new hires coming from academia to know all the details of how the field is practiced in industry. We remember the different motivations and constraints of academia. However, it is a pleasant surprise when someone we are interviewing from academia demonstrates that he or she understands there is a difference, and why that difference exists. Conversely, it is deeply annoying when an interviewee implies that the interviewers are doing their work all wrong, and could solve all of their problems just by applying the latest techniques from academia. People working in industry do keep up with their fields. If we aren't applying the latest techniques it could be because we're lazy or uninformed. It could also be because the latest techniques do not translate well to an industrial setting — or at least not yet. Regardless of the actual reason, it would be best if you assumed the latter. Insulting your interviewer is never a good interview technique.

If you do want to talk about a great new technique with an industry contact, one safe way to raise the topic is to ask about why that technique does not apply to their work. For instance, if you are curious why the smart industrial underwater basket-weaver you've just met isn't using the latest snorkel technology, you could ask: "We've had a lot of luck with Fingle's Fantastic Snorkel 2.0, but it doesn't seem to get much use in industry. Do you know why?" This indicates that you know your conversation partner is smart enough to evaluate new technology for herself, and frames the discussion as a request for information, not a judgment of her techniques.

If you are working in a field that involves technology, it is an extremely good idea to learn what professionals in the relevant technology field consider to be good practices. For instance, if you are a programmer, learn what patterns are and how they can be used. If you are a data geek, understand the theory behind relational databases. If you are looking at process science positions, learn about the method of statistical design of experiments. Learn about how people using the same technology in different applications solve problems, how they test their solutions for enterprise use, and how they ensure scalability. Not all industrial positions will require this knowledge, but it will open up additional opportunities for you. These things are not hidden, arcane knowledge. A simple web search will turn up many resources for anyone who wants to learn them. You will set yourself apart from many people migrating from academia if you have at least started to learn about these practices.

Calibrate your expectations and mindset

Prepare yourself to hear some disparaging comments about academia and how it is not "the real world" and you have not yet held a "real job." It is best to just ignore these comments and change the topic. These are indeed insulting and infuriating comments, but a job search is no time to take a moral stand on the value of academia in society. You can do that after you get a job.

You must also prepare yourself for the reality that in industry, your years in academia are translated to years of experience at a discounted rate. It can be hard to realize that after investing years in a post-graduate degree, and perhaps years more in post-doctoral research, you will have to accept a junior position in industry. However, you need to accept this before you can be successful in your non-academic job search. If you start by demanding respect for your academic credentials and experience, you are more likely to be passed over for positions. You have to recognize how much your academic background hasn't taught you, so that the skills that it has given you can be noticed.

It is okay to start in an entry level position. You have plenty of time. A career is a long thing. You'll probably advance quickly because of the skills you learned in academia, even if your new colleagues don't really see how they are relevant. Just be patient, do good work, and learn the ropes in the new field.

Don't dismiss contract work

Contract and temporary work can seem like bad options, since these positions lack job security and fringe benefits (e.g., paid time off and medical insurance). However, they can be an excellent way to get your foot in the door and prove your value to a company, and they also offer a chance to build a network of people who can vouch for the quality of your work in an industrial setting. Companies are often more likely to take a risk on a contractor than a full time hire, because if he or she doesn't work out, they can just not renew the contract rather than going through the relatively complicated and unpleasant process of firing someone.

Contract work does not have to be a financially bad choice. It should pay a higher hourly rate than an equivalent salaried full time position does, because the company is not paying benefits or payroll taxes. A full discussion of how to set your contract rate is beyond the scope of this book, but you should research this if you are targeting a field in which contract work is common.

3. Build a network

Networking is incredibly important for any non-academic job search. There is a reason that "it's not what you know, it's who you know" is an old adage. It is not that hiring managers are all heartless jerks who only want to hire friends. Most industry jobs require not just the appropriate domain skills, but also the ability to function in a corporate environment and various other traits that are hard to discern in an interview. Many hiring managers will therefore try to find someone they trust who knows the candidate and can vouch for these traits. Furthermore, hiring managers often need to review hundreds of resumes for an open position. It is difficult — if not impossible — to give every resume a thorough review. Resumes recommended by someone the hiring manager knows are likely to get extra attention.

Networking can also help you sort through often contradictory job search advice and determine which advice best applies to the specific industry you are targeting. Once you know some people in your target industry, you can ask them for their advice. This will be more valuable than any general advice you read, including this book.

Unfortunately, the heavy reliance on networking in industrial hiring can have an exclusionary effect, tending to favor people who are like the people already working at the company, to the detriment of people who belong to one or more marginalized groups. I am not arguing that this is the right way to hire, just that in my experience it is how people do hire. I absolutely agree that hiring managers should learn how to reach outside of their usual networks and companies should work to develop more inclusive hiring practices.

Until those things happen, though, the onus falls on the job seeker. Like it or not, if you want to get a non-academic job, you need to network. This is hardest to do when you're looking for your first job. Once you've had a job or two, you have a natural network of past coworkers, who (if you weren't unpleasant or unreliable) will almost certainly put in a good word for you given the chance. However, there are some steps you can take to build a network before you have worked in industry.

Prepare your elevator speech

The first step is to make sure that you can give a compelling yet brief summary of your research. This is the famed "elevator speech" that networking gurus tell you to have, except you don't have to pitch it to someone completely outside your field. Instead, come up with a summary that is appropriate for a general audience in your field. You can assume familiarity with basic concepts but not with the details and jargon of your specific field. For instance, a scientist could assume that her conversation partner would understand evolution, tectonic plates, and the fact that proteins aren't just something in bodybuilding drinks, but not that he would know the role of a specific protein in the cell cycle or the importance of the spotted owl in the ecology of a particular state. Make sure you include some idea of why anyone should care about your research. Do not start networking until you can give your research summary smoothly and succinctly!

Next, take the list of the specific types of industry jobs in which you are interested and write a short summary of those fields and why you are interested in them. This should be just a few sentences long, because you'll often want to combine it with your summary of your research, and you don't want it to seem like you're telling someone your life story just to find out if they know someone who can help you. This summary can help your networking contacts understand the logic of your job search, which will allow them to suggest other potential fields you may not have considered. It will also make it more likely that you will be seen as having a genuine interest in your targeted fields, which makes people more likely to be willing to invest time in training you, and therefore, more likely to hire you.

This process sounds more difficult than it really is. You already know what you need to say: you just need to practice saying it confidently and concisely. For instance, here is a potential elevator speech for an underwater basket-weaver hoping to find a job in industry:

"I am completing my PhD in Dr. Weaver's lab at Woven U, looking at the effects of reed preparation and snorkel selection on basket outcomes. Our aim was to decrease the overall cost per basket by reducing failures. During my research, I developed interests in snorkel design and reed engineering, and am now looking for industrial positions in which I can pursue one or both of those interests."

It really can be as short as that. This statement is intended to open a conversation, not answer all possible questions. The person to whom you are talking will pick up on the piece that is most interesting to her, and ask follow up questions.

Start networking

Now you are ready to start networking in earnest. You are not at this point networking to get a job. In fact, you should never network specifically "to get a job." You are networking to plant seeds that might grow to help you get a job at some point in your career. Right now, your main interest in networking is to learn about career options in industry and to start accumulating some contacts in industry who will be able to say to a hiring manager with an appropriate job "Hey, you should check out Josephina Bloggs. I can't vouch for her work, but I had lunch with her and she seems sharp."

Start with your current circle of friends and acquaintances, even if they are all also in academia and seem unlikely to be able to help. Let people know what you're interested in learning about, and they might have leads for you. Follow up with the people your friends recommend, and those people may have additional leads for you, and so on and so on.

You can also join industry associations and local industry networking groups. If you are a member of a group that is underrepresented in your target industry, join one or more of the relevant advocacy groups, such as the Association for Women in Science and the National Society of Black Engineers. You may need to ask around (or go to a few trial meetings) to figure out which groups are most relevant to your interests and active in your area. Go to the meetings. Talk to people. If you can, volunteer on a committee or two. If all you've done is schmooze with someone, all that person can say is that you didn't seem like a freak. This is still a valuable recommendation, but you want better, particularly in this tight market. If you've worked on a committee with someone, that person can talk about how you work in groups, your work ethic and reliability, and other relevant things.

Whether or not you choose to volunteer at an organization, go to the events and talk to the other attendees. Give them your summary about your research background and what you're interested in doing. You might meet someone who knows someone who can help, and chances are, the person you meet will offer to introduce you. If one of the speakers seems to be in a relevant field or had good advice, try to talk to him or her. The speaker may be mobbed after the talk, though, so it is often easier to talk to other attendees, and they are just as likely to be nice people with useful information or contacts.

Check your alumni associations. These organizations keep lists of alumni who have specifically indicated that they are willing to answer questions and offer advice. In my experience, this is a greatly underutilized resource. Ask your alumni office what resources they provide, and whether or not they have a database of potentially helpful alumni that you can search.

Conduct informational interviews

Once you find a contact in your target industry, you can organize an informational interview. An informational interview is an interview where you ask someone who's working in a job that sounds interesting to you a lot of questions and try to figure out if you'd like the job and how you might get such a job. You do not contact someone and ask for a job, even if that person has a job you want posted. You contact her and ask if you can ask some general questions about her field and how she got to where she is today.

This is the step where many of your peers will drop out. It is intimidating to reach out to people you do not know and ask them to meet you to answer your questions. Why in the world would they agree to do this? Amazingly, most people will say yes. They remember how hard it was to make the transition out of academia and are willing to help out. Also, people generally like to talk about themselves and to feel like an expert giving advice.

If the person you contact says no or ignores you, don't worry about it. Just move on to the next person. There are a lot of people in your target industry. You will find someone who is willing to talk to you. As long as you do not badger the person you contacted, you have done yourself no harm.

If you can't find anyone close by to ask for an interview, do the interview via email or using a videoconferencing system such as Skype. This is not likely to be as helpful as an in person meeting, but it can still be useful, particularly if you are willing to relocate for a job.

Once you've scheduled an informational interview, spend some time preparing. Do background research online so that you know the basic jargon of the field, and can ask intelligent questions. Prepare a list of questions and take it with you to the interview. You don't need an extensive list, just a few to get the conversation started. You can also always ask someone to tell you about his career path, and to describe a day in the life of someone in his job. Then let the conversation evolve. You'll probably come up with more questions as the conversation proceeds.

Again, you absolutely must be prepared to give your research summary and the summary of what sorts of industry jobs you're considering. If you can't give a good research summary, your interviewee is unlikely to want to stick her neck out and tell a potential hiring manager that she thinks you are sharp. If you can't describe the information and advice you're looking for, she can't search her network for someone who can help you.

After the interview is over, follow up with a thank you email. If the interviewee offered to put you in touch with some other people, this is a good chance to say something like "I look forward to talking to your friends Joe Jackson and Annie Anderson about opportunities in industrial underwater basket-weaving." Usually, this is enough of a reminder to prompt someone to follow through on their offer of help. If a couple of weeks pass and you never get that introduction, though, you can reach out again with a gentle reminder, saying something like "I know you're very busy. I just wanted to check if you've had a chance to contact Joe Jackson, in case I missed an email." Only remind someone once unless they have specifically told you to pester them until they follow through. If they don't follow through, heave a big sigh and move on to the next contact.

You should also ask your interviewee if you can connect on LinkedIn. This will let you search his network for help in answering future questions, and may also be helpful if a potential future boss is searching her LinkedIn network to see if she knows anyone who knows Josephina Bloggs, the candidate she is considering interviewing.

Use LinkedIn and other social media

LinkedIn is the primary social network used for professional networking. Twitter and blogs also offer opportunities to connect with people, but in my experience, they take more time to yield results. Some people try to respond helpfully to complete strangers who send emails to their blog addresses. Other people do not, and will only respond to regular commenters. In general, the more well-known the blog is, the more likely it is that the person who writes it gets a lot of requests for help, and the less likely it is that the blogger will be able to answer each request. One possible approach would be to search Twitter for topics you're interested in and see if you find anyone to follow. Follow them, and maybe reply to a few tweets when you have something relevant to say. With time, this might lead to a real connection. I think the direct networking approach is more likely to work quickly, but if you're a year or two out from needing the connections and want to explore a lot of potential fields, a Twitter-based approach might be worth trying.

If you're only going to use one social network for your job search, though, you should choose LinkedIn. LinkedIn is not magic and it will not make this brutal job market any less brutal, but it is an extremely helpful tool for a non-academic job search. In academia, there is a lot of emphasis on your formal pedigree, and you publish papers that serve as detailed calling cards for your work. People can judge the quality of your work by reading your papers. People working in industry don't usually publish as much. Most of the juicy details of their work are covered by non-disclosure agreements, so even in an interview they can't talk in depth about them. Therefore, if they want to evaluate a candidate's work before hiring him, they try to find someone whose opinion they trust who can vouch for him. This is where LinkedIn comes in.

I see LinkedIn used in four ways:

1. Hiring managers often search LinkedIn when

evaluating a resume, to see if they know anyone who knows the applicant and might be able to give an indication of whether or not to interview the applicant.

2. Job-seekers looking at a job opportunity search their network on LinkedIn to see if they have any first or second level contacts at the company of interest who can perhaps help their resumes get a little extra attention.

3. Job-seekers considering different fields or making a career change search their LinkedIn network to identify second level connections who might be good people with whom to have informational interviews. The standard procedure is to email your first level connection and ask to be introduced to the person with whom you want to have an informational interview. Since you are being introduced by someone he or she knows, the new contact is more likely to agree to a meeting.

4. People join LinkedIn groups relevant to their interests, as a way to learn from other peoples' experiences, ask for and receive advice, and build a professional reputation (by providing good answers to other members' questions). In some cases, recruiters and hiring managers may also post open positions in group discussions. As with all social media endeavors, you will get the most benefit from LinkedIn groups in which you are authentically engaged.

There is a fifth way in which LinkedIn is used that applies mainly to more senior positions: recruiters and hiring managers sometimes search public LinkedIn profiles for specific skills, looking for potential candidates for hard to fill positions. This is less likely to happen to you in the early stage of your career, but it is worth having a public LinkedIn profile to allow for this possibility.

Once you have had an industry job, you will populate your LinkedIn network with the people you worked with at that job. Your LinkedIn network will grow organically as you work with more and more people. However, when you are fresh out of academia, it is a very different story, and using LinkedIn can be a bit intimidating.

Here are some ideas for how to use LinkedIn to help transition from academia to industry:

1. Set up a profile. You want to include enough details about your experience to allow recruiters to find you via searches and to help people you've met refresh their memories about what you do, but you don't want to be so specific that you inadvertently exclude yourself from potential positions. I recommend putting a trimmed down version of your resume in your profile. List all the schools you've attended and summarize the jobs you've held, but do not go into great detail about your projects. If you are considering a range of different types of positions, keep the summary quite general. Your LinkedIn profile is something that you may find you want to revisit and revise as you gain more information about the specific industry you're targeting via informational interviews.

2. Decide how to handle the photo. As part of setting up your profile, you will need to decide whether to include a photo. Including a photo is generally recommended, because it will increase the "percent complete" score of your profile, and when someone searches LinkedIn on keywords, profiles with a higher percent complete score are listed first. A photo can also help remind people you've met at networking events who you are. However, there can be disadvantages to including a photo, too, particularly if you are a member of a group against whom discrimination commonly occurs. If you do include a photo, make sure it is appropriate for a professional network. Dress as you would for work in the field that you are targeting, and get someone to take a simple headshot.

3. Build a starting network. Search LinkedIn for your email contacts and make as many connections as you can. Search for former labmates or research collaborators and connect with them.

4. Grow your network. Some people will accept LinkedIn connection requests from people they don't know, but those are essentially useless. You only want to connect with people who will feel comfortable introducing you to someone else in their network. If they don't know you at all, chances are they won't make the introduction. You can still grow your network by connecting with new people you meet. For instance, after you go to a conference or networking event, send connection requests to people you met. Only

send invitations to people with whom you had a conversation. Don't spam everyone on the conference list. Customize the connection request email to remind the person where you met him. LinkedIn has been streamlining the process of sending connection requests, and in some contexts you will not get the chance to customize your request. You may want to take notes on the method of sending connection requests that works best for you.

5. Keep it professional. Only link your Twitter account or blog to LinkedIn if you primarily write about things that are relevant to work. Don't connect things to your LinkedIn account that aren't about work.

6. Search your second level network (your connections' connections) for help. When you're just starting out, look for people with whom you can have informational interviews. Remember to connect with them on LinkedIn after the interview. I have recommended someone I met through an informational interview for an open position at a friend's company. It is rare, but it happens. I had not kept in close contact with the person with whom I had an informational interview, so would not have been able to find that person if I didn't have a LinkedIn connection.

7. Search for relevant LinkedIn groups. Pick a small number in which to engage. Become active in the discussions by asking and answering questions. Keep your posts authentic, but avoid direct self-promotion. This approach will require time and patience to

provide results, so only do this if you are willing to invest that time and be patient.

Whatever social media you choose to use in relation to your job search, remember that you will get the most benefit if you engage authentically, with the intention of connecting with other people, learning from them, and sharing your own expertise where appropriate. Frequent, blatant self-promotion is rarely a winning strategy on any social media platform.

Also void posting bitter rants on social media or engaging in "flame wars." People will often remember the venom long after they forget who was in the right. Be sure that you are willing to accept the consequences of anything you post being read by a potential employer.

Maintain your network

Networking is a task on your job search "to do" list that you can never check off as completed. In fact, it is something that you should expect to do continuously throughout your career. You may spend more time and energy on it during periods when you are actively searching for a new job, but for your network to be most effective, you cannot ignore it when you're not looking, either.

Some people advise trying to connect with each person in your network once a month. I do not think that is necessary, or even realistic in this age of large online networks. However, if you come across an article that makes you think of someone you've met, don't hesitate to send it to him with a short note about how it brought to mind the conversation you had last time you saw each other. Try to at least say hello to people you already know when you see them at industry events, even if your main focus is meeting new people.

Another good method for maintaining your network is to arrange occasional lunches with the people in your network you know well. It is best not to leave this until you need help from them, but since most people tend to ignore their networks until they need help, most people are understanding of the fact that you are more likely to reach out to them when you are looking for career help. If you have neglected a networking contact for months or even years, and now think there is something she might be able to do to help you, go ahead and reach out. As long as your last interaction was a positive one, most people will still try to help.

Conversely, be as generous as you can be when other people reach out to you for help, even people who are junior to you. There are several people I meet with frequently whom I first met when they asked me for career advice, and who now have advanced to a position in their careers in which they can sometimes provide me with useful contacts or information. People grow and change, and we tend to remember the people who helped us on our own paths.

You may be thinking that networking sounds like it requires you to expend a lot of effort to end up in social interactions that you are likely to find at least a little bit awkward. This is true. However, as you network more often, the interactions will feel less awkward, and will require less effort to arrange. Some networking contacts may become warm acquaintances or even true friends. Regardless of whether this happens, networking is worth the effort. Building and maintaining a solid network will help your career in ways you cannot predict, as people in your network think of you for opportunities you might never have otherwise considered pursuing. It is possible to have a good career without doing any networking. However, I can almost guarantee that you will have a better career if you invest some time and effort in networking.

PART II: APPLY FOR JOBS

You've identified a position for which you want to apply. Now what? Don't just grab your standard resume and submit it. You are much more likely to be successful if you take the time to customize your application materials. This section will describe how to do that.

1. Network. Again.

Don't apply for a job before you search your network (e.g., LinkedIn) to see if you know someone at that organization who might be able to put in a good word for you and/or hand your resume to the hiring manager. It is much better to send your resume in via someone who will provide a personal recommendation than to just submit via the online form. You will usually be asked to submit via the online form, too, but send your resume in via your connection first. In some larger companies, all resumes that come in through the website are triaged by someone in the human resources department. This person may or may not know anything about the field in which you work, and sometimes your resume is weeded out simply because you used slightly different words to describe your skills than the hiring manager did when describing the position to the human resources department. If you can get your resume directly to the hiring manager, you can avoid this problem.

Submitting your resume directly to the hiring manager may also make your resume seem like a "find" and therefore garner it more attention. This is a bit sad — it shouldn't matter how the resume lands on a hiring manager's stack. Unfortunately, though, it can matter, so if you have a connection to a position, use it. Also, if your connection submits your resume, he or she might get a referral bonus, which will certainly generate some goodwill.

If you cannot find a connection at the company, do not give up on the job. Prepare your resume and cover letter and submit them via the standard process, anyway. People do occasionally get hired from the pool of online resume submissions.

2. Write a great resume

You should convert your academic Curriculum Vitae (CV) into an industry resume. An academic CV is a complete listing of your past experiences. Industry resumes are more focused. Although it is rare to omit a past position completely, it is common and expected to condense the information about positions that are not particularly relevant to the one for which you are currently applying. Using the correct format will increase your chances of catching a hiring manager's attention and greatly help anyone who has offered to keep an eye out for relevant positions for you. Your resume presents a view of your skills and experiences that emphasizes how you fit the needs of the position. This is usually your first opportunity to shape how the hiring manager views you, so it is worth the effort to make sure that the view she receives is the one you intend to transmit.

The following is a section by section overview of a standard industry resume, which will help you create an initial resume. Resume expectations vary by industry, though, so it is a good idea to get your initial resume reviewed by someone in your target industry. Every time you apply for a job, you should also customize your resume for that specific job. Tips for customization are included in the section overviews below.

Profile or objective

A resume usually includes either an objective or a profile at the top. Whether you choose to use a profile or an objective is a matter of personal preference. I personally prefer a profile because I think the objective is fairly self-evident (my objective is to get the job for which I'm applying!) but in my years as a hiring manager, I've seen a roughly equal mix of the two, and as long as the section is well-written, I don't think it matters which form you use. The profile is also sometimes called a summary. This distinction is utterly meaningless.

The objective or profile section is a written version of the elevator speech you developed for networking purposes, tailored for the job for which you are applying. It should be only one to three sentences long. It is absolutely essential that you tailor this section. Sending in a resume with a profile that does not fit the position for which you are applying will greatly decrease your chances of being called for an interview, because not only have you implied that your true interests lie elsewhere, but you've also demonstrated a lack of attention to detail. If you cannot tailor this section for each position, it would be better to omit it altogether.

If you are sending the resume to a networking contact who has offered to help you, you should try to craft a version that can plausibly cover all of the types of jobs in which you might be interested. This is hard to write. I struggle with it every single time I run a job search. It is worth doing, though, because this is the first thing people looking at your resume see, and it gives them the reference frame into which they will fit the rest of your resume.

Here is what a summary or profile might look like for someone who is just starting out:

Scientist with interdisciplinary experience in basket-weaving and snorkeling, strong technical skills in reed preparation and snorkel selection, and demonstrated ability to master new weaving techniques quickly.

Here is what an objective might look like for the same junior underwater basket-weaver:

To obtain an entry-level position in underwater basket-weaving in which I can apply my interdisciplinary snorkeling and weaving experience, strong reed preparation and snorkel selection skills, and learn new weaving techniques.

You should tweak the order of the clauses and include or exclude specific skills and experiences based on the job for which you are applying. If you have one of the key skills that the job description lists, try to get it in this section. If you could plausibly apply for multiple types of jobs, have a different summary or profile for each type. For instance, I have moved among jobs that are more science-oriented, more technology-oriented, and more management-oriented throughout my career. When I apply for a job now, I use my profile section to emphasize the part of my experience that is most relevant to the particular job for which I am applying.

Key skills

There is some debate about whether the key skills section should go right after your summary/objective or at the end of the resume. There is no one right answer. My personal bias is to put it after the summary for more technical positions, and move it to the end when applying for management positions. I've seen it in all sorts of locations, though, and I personally have never cared where I find it in an applicant's resume. I definitely want to see this section, though, particularly for more junior positions.

The key skills section is exactly what it sounds like: a listing of your key skills. The combination of this section and your profile is the "too long; didn't read" version of your resume. When I am filling a position, I read the profile and the key skills, and then decide how carefully to read the rest of the resume. This sounds harsh, but remember that I review hundreds of resumes for any position I post. Hiring managers have to use something to decide which resumes are worth more attention, and using the profile and key skills is better than using the formatting and font choice.

Only list skills in which you have reasonably strong proficiency. Do not list things that you know about from reading a paper or two or in which you have only dabbled. If those things are truly relevant to the job, mention them in your cover letter, not here. Stretching the truth in this section will likely disqualify your application. If I interview someone who does not turn out to have the skills he or she listed, I will not hire that person, end of story.

It is best to divide this section into bullet points, arranged by type of skill. For instance, here is what our basket weaver might have:

- **Basket-weaving:** cross weave, Thompson's anti-fray weave, reed preparation
- **Diving:** snorkel selection, Jones' free dive technique
- **Basket-finishing:** advanced decorative design, design testing

Professional experience

This section is the main body of the resume, in which you summarize your work experience, in reverse chronological order. For someone just leaving academia, I recommend listing any post-doctoral positions (including lectureships or professorships), your graduate research assistant position, and any relevant experience from before graduate school. If you worked between college and graduate school, list what you did, even if it is not directly relevant. If it isn't relevant, it is fine to make it a very short entry, but don't leave it out, or the hiring manager might assume something bad was happening during that time period. If you have an extended break (one year or more) during which you have nothing to put on your resume, briefly mention what you were doing in your cover letter.

I would only include part-time positions you held during college if they are relevant, e.g., research work or a position in which you garnered some supervisory experience. However, this is truly an area for which there are no right answers and standard practice varies quite a bit by industry. Your best course of action is to find someone in your target industry and get his or her opinion.

Don't list jobs you held in high school or between high school and college unless you had an amazing and relevant internship or other experience relevant to the position to which you are applying. I scooped ice cream at an ice cream parlor and sold popcorn at a movie theater in high school. No one cared about that, even when I was fresh out of graduate school, and I didn't do a postdoctoral fellowship, so my resume was light for that first job application.

Include a job title, the date range, and a very brief summary of the job (e.g., "responsibility for all lab basket-weaving. Hired and managed two technicians.") before listing three to six specific accomplishments for the job. In general you should list more accomplishments for the more recent positions. You should also customize your resume for different jobs by including more detail about older experiences if it is relevant to the job requirements.

Be specific when you describe your work experience. Don't just state that you were a research assistant in the Jones Underwater Basket-Weaving Lab. Pick the most significant work you did as a research assistant and list those specific tasks or projects as bullet points. The standard advice is to make these bullet points action and result oriented. Don't just list what you did: list how it benefited your employer and try to quantify that benefit. I think this is difficult for most people without much industry experience, but you are likely to find at least some bullet points that you can rework into this style. For example, you could turn this:

- Designed novel 5-point basket weave to improve fish capturing capacity.

Into this:

- Designed novel 5-point basket weave, resulting in 4-fold increase in average fish catch.

Or perhaps even better:

- Increased average fish catch 4-fold by designing a novel 5-point basket weave.

Whatever you do, don't just say:

- Designed novel 5-point basket weave.

That is boring, and casts doubt on whether you understand the practical applications of your work.

If you choose to include teaching experience in this section, try to translate that experience into bullets that show your talents in training other people. Most industry positions eventually involve training someone else in something you have mastered, so teaching experience can certainly be relevant. However, a listing that simply states that you were a teaching assistant does not tell the hiring manager much useful information about your work experience. If all you want to say about your teaching experience is that you have it, list it briefly in a separate section.

Education

Some people put the education section right after the key skills. I put it after the experience section, but I am much further away from my educational experiences than someone who is just starting out. I don't think it really matters whether it is after key skills or experience, particularly for someone just leaving academia. However, I do think it is a bit odd when the first thing someone who has some post-graduate experience wants me to see on their resume is where they got their degree.

In this section, you should list all of the degrees that you have obtained, in reverse chronological order. When you are relatively junior, you can flesh out your resume by including the title and a summary for any undergraduate thesis you wrote. As you get more senior, you'll drop the undergraduate thesis but keep the information for your graduate thesis (although you'll probably keep trimming it to make more room for your professional accomplishments). If you are applying for a research position or a position in a field largely populated by people with PhDs, list your graduate advisor or advisors. Don't bother listing your high school education. No one cares where you went to high school, even if it was a wonderful school with an excellent reputation. In most cases, your college and graduate school grade point averages are irrelevant, too.

If you have taken any additional formal training that is relevant, list it. For instance, if an underwater basket-weaver has taken a training course from the manufacturer of a particular reed harvesting system, she would list that course. She would not generally list individual courses taken in the pursuit of her degree, though.

Massive open online courses (MOOCs) are too recent a development for there to be a standard practice on their inclusion in resumes. Listing relevant MOOCs might be helpful for someone attempting a transition into a new field. Certainly only list them if they are relevant: if I am hiring a scientific programmer, I don't care that the applicant completed a MOOC about Greek myths.

Awards

List any awards you have received, reaching back to college but not before. This is another section that slowly dwindles over the course of your career, and it is not unusual to see awards listed with the relevant educational or professional experience, rather than in their own section. If you are applying for a position in which the ability to secure grants is important, you should make sure to include all awards and grants that you won via a submission process. Otherwise, I would not worry much about this section, as it is unlikely to have much impact on whether or not you get an interview.

Patents, publications and presentations

List patents, publications, and presentations, much as you would for an academic CV. This can be a separate page (or pages!) and does not count against the usual two to three page length for a resume. Consider putting your name in bold in the authors list for each publication, to make it easier for the person who is reviewing the resume to find you.

Other tips

Your resume should be at most two to three pages without publications. This probably won't be a problem during your early career, but might be challenging as you become more senior. Do the work to trim your resume down to size. Most hiring managers I know are annoyed by long resumes, not impressed. Keep what is relevant to the position for which you are applying, condense or drop what is not. Similarly, do not pad your resume if it is less than two pages. This will also not impress the hiring manager, who will now need to hunt through the extraneous information to find the skills for which he is looking.

You really must customize your resume for each and every job for which you apply. You are not telling your entire professional life story. You are presenting a particular view of that story that emphasizes how it matches the job posting to which you are responding.

Finally, have someone proofread your resume, even if you are a native English speaker. Some hiring managers will overlook a typo or two, but other hiring managers are really annoyed by them. Grammatical errors and sentences that don't make sense will almost always count against you. Remember, the person reading your resume is going to be reading many, many emails and reports from you if you are hired. No one is enthusiastic about struggling through incomprehensible written communication.

3. Write a compelling cover letter

A cover letter is an intimidating thing to write. For many people, it is the hardest part of a job application. It certainly is for me, and I've written dozens of cover letters and read hundreds of them. The basics of what you need to do aren't difficult to grasp, but it can be very hard to write something that covers those basics well and still feels authentic. However, you should always include a cover letter if at all possible, and it is worth investing considerable effort in writing it. A good cover letter can rescue an otherwise mediocre application.

A bad cover letter, on the other hand, can completely sink your chances for the job. Bad cover letters I've received as a hiring manager include letters that indicate the applicant has a life-long interest in some field other than the one involved in the job, letters that are riddled with spelling and grammatical errors, and letters that I have to reread several times in order to comprehend.

Those are easy mistakes to avoid. However, most cover letters are not bad, but they're not good. They don't really hurt your chances, but they don't help them. To me, there are three basic requirements for a good cover letter:

1. Convey the right information
2. Use clear, concise writing
3. Use proper grammar.

The next sections will examine each component, one at a time.

Convey the right information

A cover letter should not simply regurgitate all of the information in your resume in paragraph form. Instead, the cover letter should highlight the most relevant portions of the resume, draw attention to the growth of your key skills over the course of your career, and provide context when it is needed.

The purpose of a cover letter is to summarize how your skills and experience match the key skills in the job posting. You need to do the work of mapping your skills to the skills the hiring manager has stated that she wants. Use the keywords from the job ad: don't make the hiring manager construct the map from your skills to her requirements, and don't make her guess if your "aqueous container construction" is the same thing as the "underwater basket-weaving experience" requested in her posting, even if you come from an academic environment that strongly prefers the term "aqueous container construction."

You should not laboriously map every single skill in the job posting to your background. Instead, pick the key skills. This is a chance to demonstrate that you truly understand the position and what the key skills for that position might be. If you read a job posting and can't figure out what the key skills are, you should try to do more research into that field. It is probably a very poorly written job posting, but unfortunately, it is up to you to deal with that and work around it to submit a solid application anyway.

If there is a significant hole in your background with respect to the posting, don't pretend it isn't there and think the hiring manager won't notice. The hiring manager is almost certainly scanning cover letters and resumes specifically looking for the key skills — if yours is missing too many of those skills, it will just be skipped. Instead, think hard about your background and experience, and try to identify something that indicates an aptitude for learning the missing skill. For instance, let's say the job description calls for experience in underwater basket-weaving, coordinated diving techniques, and reed selection. You have solid experience in underwater basket-weaving and coordinated diving techniques, but lack direct experience in reed selection. However, you collaborated on a project in which you worked with the reed selection group. You can say something like this:

"While I do not have direct experience in reed selection, I collaborated closely with the reed selection department on a basket diversification initiative at Woven University, which gave me exposure to the fundamental properties that must be considered when selecting reeds for an underwater basket-weaving project."

This is particularly powerful if you can offer to put the hiring manager in touch with the person with whom you collaborated, and that person will say you are wonderful. The above paragraph, by the way, is a heavily anonymized real life example, in which I hired someone who had absolutely no experience in one of the key areas of the job. The cover letter sold me on the candidate, and the hire worked out beautifully.

You can only use this technique if you have some past experience that truly indicates an aptitude. Do not contort your experience into unnatural configurations to try to make a connection that just isn't there. If you do not have anything at all relevant in your background and the missing skill is one of the key aspects of the job, say something like this:

"While I have not yet gained direct experience in reed selection, I look forward to the chance to grow in this area."

Other things to include in a cover letter, if relevant are:

An explanation of any unusual gaps in your work experience, particularly if they are recent. This can be very brief. If you have a gap due to child rearing or elder care, simply state that. If this will be your first job after the gap and you can point to something you've done to stay current or refresh your skills, do so. If it is not your first position after the gap (for instance, if you spent several years after graduate school raising children, but then completed a postdoctoral fellowship), you may not want to mention the gap at all, and instead focus on the skills gained in the post-doctoral position. Handling a gap due to child care is difficult, because many managers still have biases against mothers (and motherhood is not a protected employment class) and stay at home fatherhood is still a rare enough choice to evoke comment. However, if there is a recent, noticeable gap on your resume, it is usually better to address it.

You usually do not need to explain a gap between college and graduate school, unless it is unusually long (more than a year or so). However, if you are doing a postdoctoral fellowship now and had a gap between graduate school and the fellowship, you should explain that.

If you are changing fields, indicate that you are interested in the new field. You cannot assume that your interest in the new field is obvious. Maybe you've just fundamentally misunderstood the job posting. Maybe you are applying to any feasible posting in certain target companies in hopes of making an internal transfer later. The hiring manager cannot read your mind, and you should not assume he will give you the benefit of the doubt. This can be a single sentence, such as: "I am interested in the chance to apply my knowledge of basket types to applications in underwater basket-weaving." This indicates that you have read and understood that the job is not in the history and classification of basket types, and that you are at least willing to claim an interest in the new field beyond the potential to collect a paycheck. If your only interest in the new field is to collect a paycheck or you are indeed hoping to use this position as a stepping stone to an internal transfer, it is best to keep that to yourself.

Immigration status, if it is in your favor. If you have a name or educational background that will make people assume you might need sponsorship in order to work in the United States, you may want to clarify that in the cover letter. In general, I would only do this if you can clarify it to state that you do not need sponsorship. If you do need sponsorship, I would not mention your immigration status at all. If the hiring manager is interested in hiring you, he will ask about this at the stage in the process when his company's policies tell him to do so.

Use clear, concise writing

Most corporate jobs involve a lot of writing. If nothing else, you are likely to be writing many emails. No one willingly signs up for a future of reading someone else's tortured prose. You want your cover letter to convince the hiring manager that you can write well. This does not mean that your writing must be on a par with that of a great novelist, but you must be able to structure your paragraphs and sentences logically and convey your message concisely.

Your cover letter must not be long and rambling, but it also must be long enough to convey all of the necessary information. Aim for three paragraphs of three to four sentences each. That is a guideline, not a rule. If you can cover all of the important information in less space, do so. Think carefully before writing a longer letter, though.

Remember that the recipient is reading hundreds of them.

Your cover letter absolutely must be constructed logically. If the hiring manager cannot follow your letter without serious effort, she is probably not going to hire you.

Since the cover letter functions as a writing sample, I disagree with the advice I sometimes see to make a table mapping skills in the job description to specific items in your background. However, I would be unlikely to rule out a candidate for doing this, so if you are a very weak writer, you can consider that method. I think it would be better to get some writing advice, instead, but perhaps if you are applying for a very technical job, the writing sample aspect is less important. If you want to use this format, try to find someone in your target industry to ask for advice. Even if you do not use this as the final format, writing a table mapping your skills to those requested in the job description can help you organize your thoughts for the cover letter and will also help you prepare for an interview.

Use proper grammar

Hiring managers may be reasonably forgiving of a typo or two in the resume and cover letter, but a true grammatical mistake is usually a mark against the candidate. I am more forgiving in this regard if the candidate is not a native English speaker, but even then I will not overlook a large number of mistakes. Find a native speaker to proofread your writing. If you do not have a friend who will do this, look for paid help.

The reason I so strongly dislike grammatical mistakes in cover letters is simple: it shows a lack of attention to detail and precision, and those are usually things I need the person I am hiring to have. Writing a cover letter and resume is a good time to get in touch with your inner perfectionist.

Other tips

When you apply to multiple jobs at a single company, the hiring managers can almost certainly see this, even if the company is quite large. The resume tracking systems companies use make this obvious.

There is nothing inherently wrong with applying for a couple of closely related jobs. In this case, you will need to work to craft a single cover letter that it is appropriate for all of the jobs for which you apply. In some cases, the resume management system will only store one. Even if you can submit more than one, they sometimes get mixed up. And even if they don't get mixed up, the hiring manager might read both. I'd therefore recommend writing a slightly more generic cover letter that can fit both jobs.

Better yet, though, would be to use your network to find someone at the company who can help you figure out which job is the best fit for you, and apply for that one job and only that job. If the people inside the company think a different job is more appropriate for you, they will probably consider you for it anyway.

Another thing to keep in mind is that preferences for cover letter styles and content vary a bit between industries, so if you can find someone in the industry you are targeting to review your cover letter and resume it is likely to be extremely helpful.

4. Give an impressive interview

If your cover letter and resume convince the hiring

manager to interview you, take a minute to congratulate yourself — and then start preparing for the interview. Usually, you will be competing against a handful of other candidates at this point and once you reach the interview stage, it is the interview that matters most in the hiring decision. Your amazing resume and cover letter are unlikely to compensate for a flubbed interview.

The details of interviewing vary widely in different industries and jobs. If none of my other arguments have convinced you that you should be networking and conducting informational interviews, maybe this will. The only way to find out what is expected in an interview in the industry you're trying to enter is to ask someone in that industry.

Even within an industry, there is a fair amount of variation from company to company. The best advice I can give on preparing for an interview is therefore to try to be well-rested and ready to think on your feet. Still, here are some pointers that might be useful:

Be prepared to demonstrate that you know what you say you know

If you are applying for a hands-on technical job, you might be asked to demonstrate your technical skills. It is particularly common to be asked to take a code test if you are applying for a job that involves programming.

Even if there is no actual test, you will probably be asked questions that attempt to confirm that you know the things your resume indicates you know. Never try to fake your way through a technical answer. If you do not know the answer, just say so, and outline the steps you would take to learn that information if you needed it on the job. Also never inflate your role in a project when asked for details about something on your resume. It is dishonest to do so, and you never know who the person asking the questions knows. I was once interviewed by the wife of a coauthor on a paper that resulted from one of my graduate school rotation projects. I'd never met her, and her last name was not the same as his, so I had no idea who she was when I was interviewing. However, she'd asked her husband about the project before the interview, and would have caught me in an instant if I'd tried to pretend my role had been bigger than it was. I didn't inflate my role, and she told me who she was. We had a laugh about the smallness of the world. I got the job, and look back on that job as one of my all-time favorite jobs. It is a good thing I didn't let a mistaken need to look more important on the project destroy that interview!

Know the basics about the company but be prepared to ask questions to learn more

Make sure you've read the company's website and know the basics about what the company does. Do a web search, too, and see if you can find any articles or other information about the company.

Come prepared with three to five questions to ask during the course of the interview. You want to have good, interesting questions for two reasons: (1) it shows curiosity and engagement, which are good things to show in an interview, and (2) you should be using the interview to determine whether or not the job is a good fit for you, and the best way to do this is to ask some questions.

You should put in the effort to figure out what you want to know about each company. However, you can always ask your interviewer to tell you about what it is like to work at that company. If your interview involves several individual one-on-one meetings, it can be particularly informative to ask multiple interviewers this question and compare their answers. I would not delve deeply into this topic during the interview, though. Ask the general question and note the answer, but be careful about asking follow up questions about specific work culture issues such as the usual number of working hours, unless the concern is a deal-breaker for you. It is very easy to convey the wrong impression about your own adaptability in these discussions.

Prepare to answer "soft skills" questions

"Soft skills" is a catch-all term for work skills that involve interpersonal interactions. If you are interviewing for a position that involves management of people or projects, you will almost certainly field a lot of these sorts of questions. In fact, I would be nervous about a company that didn't ask any questions about management style and methods during an interview for a managerial position. Unless the interviewer is a former colleague who knows me well, the failure to ask me about this would be a big red flag to me, possibly indicating that the company doesn't know what management is and why they need someone who knows how to do it.

Even if you are interviewing for a non-managerial role, you will probably be asked a couple of these questions, particularly about how you handle conflict at work. They might be questions like:

- Tell me about a time you had to work with a difficult colleague
- How would you handle it if you had a disagreement on technical approach with a coworker?

You can find more example questions online, but I think the best preparation is just to think about how you handle conflict and how you want to handle conflict, and be ready to talk about this, with a couple of specific examples in mind. This will allow you to react to any version of this question. In my experience, most of the soft skills questions are variations on the question of how you handle conflict.

Another common soft skills question is the clichéd "tell me about your biggest weakness" question. You should practice an answer to this question, because you'll almost certainly run into it. Pick something that is actually a weakness but not an irredeemable one and talk about how you mitigate its impact on your work. I never ask this question myself, but I've been in panel interviews where it has been used. I've seen perfectionism and difficulty letting go of a project used as weaknesses to good effect. I have used my tendency to get buried in operational details, and I talk about how I specifically set aside time on my calendar to pull myself out of the operational details and think about broader, more strategic issues. Note the form of that answer: as a middle manager, I'm supposed to be buried in operational details, but I should also be working to think strategically as I look ahead to future growth, and I am most effective at my job when I have a clear view of the bigger picture of what my department and company are trying to do. I've picked a real trait of mine that has aspects that make it a weakness, but that has positive aspects as well, and I've said how I mitigate the weakness aspects. You'll need to think hard about what trait you can use. You cannot convincingly copy an answer from anyone else.

Know what you want in a job and be ready to talk about it

You will probably be asked to describe your perfect job, or where you want to be in five years, or something else like this. These are hard questions, since you want to sound ambitious, but not so ambitious that you give the impression that you view the current job as nothing more than a stepping stone. Also, it is really none of the interviewer's business what you want to be doing in five years — he can't guarantee you a job in five years, after all!

Still, you need to answer the question professionally. I usually answer these questions by talking about the main qualities that make me happy in a job: feeling like I am learning new things and feeling like I am making a valuable contribution. These are my happiness criteria. If you decide to answer the question in this way, you should think about what yours are and use those.

An interview is not a confession. You need to be honest, but you do not have to tell the interviewer everything about yourself. For instance, I have a third criterion for happiness in a job. I strongly dislike a confrontational, adversarial, or overtly competitive environment, even one in which the confrontation is not meant to imply disrespect. However, I don't usually talk about that in an interview, because it can easily lead to misunderstandings about my comfort with people disagreeing with my ideas and can reinforce negative stereotypes about me as a woman. I do try to determine the company's culture during the interview, and if pushed about what I like in a culture, I talk about valuing strong teamwork, which is the positive corollary of my dislike of an adversarial environment.

Dress appropriately but in something in which you feel comfortable and confident

Dress expectations vary widely by industry (yet another reason to find a contact within your target industry to provide specific advice), but in general, if in doubt, dress more formally. I always wear a jacket, because I think a well-tailored jacket is flattering on me, so it allows me not to worry about my appearance. I'm in a somewhat casual industry, so I don't always wear a full suit, but I have on occasion.

I think it is unfortunate that we judge people on their attire and I try to minimize that tendency in myself, but in reality you will be judged on your appearance, and not everyone even fights the tendency to do so. It is therefore worth spending some effort to get your attire "right." In general, that means that women have to worry more than we'd like about the length of skirt and the cut of shirt (another reason I wear a jacket). I think nice trousers are fine, and I've interviewed in them. In some industries, though, the more conservative older men will frown upon trousers on a woman, and expect skirt suits worn with pantyhose. Regardless of your outfit, your hair and makeup (if any) should be neat and in a style appropriate for a business setting, not a social event.

Men generally have an easier time in this regard. You can almost always do fine by wearing a nice suit, or a dress shirt and nice trousers in more casual industries. You do need to make sure your suit actually fits, though, particularly if you are going with a double-breasted jacket. An ill-fitting suit is noticeable and distracting at best. At worst, some interviewers will interpret it as the dreaded "lack of attention to detail." Men with long hairstyles should make sure their hair is neat for an interview. If you usually wear your hair loose, you may want to pull it back into a low ponytail, particularly if interviewing in a more conservative industry.

People who are gender nonconforming must make a difficult decision about how much to change their attire to accommodate expectations based on gender norms. I do not have any specific advice in this area, but have read advice from others that it is best to try to find the most conforming attire in which you are comfortable.

Expectations about appropriate attire for an interview can also be challenging for people on a limited budget. Many cities have charities that work to provide people with appropriate interview clothes, so if you cannot afford the clothes you need and cannot find someone from whom you can borrow, you could try searching for one of these charities.

In general, your goal when dressing for an interview is to have your attire be absolutely not noteworthy. You want interviewers to focus on your ideas and experience, and not on your appearance. This is undeniably easier for some people to achieve than others, and can be a particularly fraught area for people who belong to a group that is underrepresented in their target industry. While someone in the majority group can get away with more flair in their attire, and in fact will sometimes be advised that will make them more memorable, people in underrepresented groups are usually best served by dressing to blend in.

Decide ahead of time how you'll handle inappropriate questions

If you are in a protected class (as defined by anti-discrimination law) you'll probably get an inappropriate question or two over the course of a job search. Actually, I suspect that in the United States, if you are anything but a white American man, you'll get an inappropriate question or two. Perhaps white male Canadians will get a pass, but the rest of us are likely to be asked things that the interviewer shouldn't ask.

Over the course of my career, I've been asked about my marriage plans, my plans to have children, and how I handle child care arrangements. There was also one memorable interview in which I was asked if I'd gone into my field to meet men. (I answered "No" and then said nothing more and waited for the next question. I did not get that job.)

There are also well-intentioned questions that stray into difficult territory. When I was interviewing while my oldest child was still a baby, one person asked me what I did for fun. The honest answer right then was that I slept for fun. (I stammered a moment, then answered that I spent my free time with my child, but also enjoyed playing music and reading. I got that job.)

There is no great way to handle these questions, and everyone has to figure out their own boundaries. Many men have no idea that women generally try not to talk about family when interviewing — they are completely unaware of the fact that research shows that there is a motherhood penalty and fatherhood bonus. They have never experienced any negative impact from discussing their family at work, so they don't think these are potentially harmful questions for a woman. Some people are just bigoted jerks and are trying to trip you up. Some people view themselves as strictly fair and honestly think that these questions are relevant and that they need to know the answers. The optimal answer will depend on which category the interviewer is in, and of course you have no way of knowing that.

Personally, I generally answer honestly but briefly and with as little detail as I can. If I am then hired into the company, I may tell someone in the Human Resources department about the experience, so that they can provide more interview training. I don't generally mention the inappropriate question at the time of the interview, because this introduces the risk of a lawsuit if the company fails to hire me, and is therefore awkward, to say the least.

Other people might prefer to decline to answer. Be aware that the more clueless interviewers are likely to be very confused by this and you might find yourself in the awkward position of explaining why those questions aren't appropriate, so include that in what you practice ahead of time.

Other tips

In many industries, it is common to hold a phone interview before deciding to bring a candidate in for an on-site interview. This is particularly common if the on-site interview will involve travel. In some companies, the phone interview is a formality, and almost everyone who has a phone interview will be brought in for an on-site interview. In other companies, it is a true screening interview and only a fraction of those called will be brought in.

You cannot know ahead of time which type of interview it is, so prepare for any phone interview as if it were a screening interview. Also, be sure that you are able to hold the interview uninterrupted, on a phone with good reception and in an environment in which you can speak freely.

It is nice to follow up after the interview with a thank you email or even a paper thank you note. It might make a good impression on the people who interviewed you, but I have never seen this have any impact on the hiring decision. This is another area in which expectations vary quite a bit in different industries, so ask your contacts in your target industry for best practices. If in doubt, err on the side of sending at least a short thank you email to your main contact at the company.

PART III: FINAL THOUGHTS

Searching for a job is difficult and stressful. It also involves a surprising amount of work and requires you to develop new skills and draw on strengths you did not think you had. It can be demoralizing and seems almost perfectly designed to undermine your self-confidence. I personally find that the best way to handle the demoralizing aspect of a job search is to have a plan for my search, and to always be working on multiple possibilities. It can be devastating to think you have found the perfect job, and then learn that the hiring manager does not think you are the right candidate for that position. It is even more devastating to have this happen when you have no other leads or other job search activities on which to focus your attention. So you should never stop your search until you have a signed contract in hand. One of the most common job search mistakes is to quit too soon.

Another common mistake is to wait too long to start a job search. Finding a job can take months, even in a strong economy. Having a solid network of contacts in your target industry can shorten the time it takes to find a job, but building that network can take years. In some ways, it is never too early to start a job search, because it is never too early to start building a network. However, I personally don't think of most networking as job hunting. Instead, I think of it as talking to interesting people about their work and my work, and I try to keep an open mind about how I might use my skills and experience in future work. Then, when it is time to look for a new job, I can think back over what I've learned from the various people I've met, and perhaps decide to pursue opportunities that I had not previously considered.

No doubt at least some of the advice in this book will require you to do things that are outside of your comfort zone. You must find a way to convince yourself to do them anyway. One way to do this is to set yourself small, concrete goals. For instance, if networking is something you tend to avoid, use the advice in this book as a starting point to break down the larger task of "networking" into smaller tasks such as "attend networking event" and "send email requesting an informational interview to person I met at the last event," then decide you will do one networking task per week, and hold yourself to that goal.

As discussed earlier, you will almost certainly face more professional rejection than you think you can handle. At times when the rejection seems particularly harsh, fall back on the techniques you developed for handling it and move on. Remember that you are making a professional transition unlike any you've previously made. The people around you may not understand what you are trying to do, and may even be actively hostile towards your new goals, because they fear what your goals say about their own choices. This is all understandably disheartening, but you must not wallow in that.

No amount of advice will make conducting a job search easy. I hope that this short book has given you some new ideas about how to approach a non-academic search, though, and will help you avoid some of the more common pitfalls. I wish you the best of luck in your search.

PART IV: NOTES AND ADDITIONAL RESOURCES

Here are some additional resources on some of the topics the book mentions:

On using LinkedIn Groups:
http://www.socialmediaexaminer.com/how-to-network-using-linkedin-groups/

A resource for general job searching advice:
http://www.askamanager.org/

On interviewing when you are not gender conforming:
http://www.butchwonders.com/blog/suits-were-purchased-pearls-were-worn

Organizations that can help with interview attire:
http://www.careergear.org/ (men)
http://dressforsuccess.org/ (women)

On the motherhood penalty:
http://curt-rice.com/2011/12/08/the-motherhood-penalty-its-not-children-that-slow-mothers-down/

On the fatherhood bonus:
http://curt-rice.com/2011/12/14/the-fatherhood-bonus-have-a-child-and-advance-your-career/

There are also many books written about general job searching. Some of that advice will apply to your specific search, some will not. The intent of this short book was not to replace those longer books, but to give a brief overview of the most important topics, so that even someone who cannot or will not spend the time on a longer book can avoid the most common pitfalls in a non-academic job search. If you find that you want to know more about any of the topics covered, definitely look for one of the longer books — or, better yet, use your networking skills to find someone in your target industry with whom you can have an informational interview.

ABOUT THE AUTHOR

M.R. Nelson is a manager of people and projects in the biotechnology industry, specializing in the intersection of science and information technology. She has more than ten years of experience as a hiring manager, and a Ph.D. in the biosciences. She is also the author of *Taming the Work Week: Work Smarter Not Longer*, a short ebook about improving personal productivity. You can find her online at BeyondManaging.com.